PROMPT DESIGN - HOW TO TALK TO AI

Unleash your AI Advantage: Effective Prompting for Better Results

Sebastian Podesser

Copyright © 2023 Sebastian Podesser

All rights reserved

No part of this book may be reproduced, or stored in a retrieval system, or transmitted in any form or by any means, electronic, mechanical, photocopying, recording, or otherwise, without express written permission of the publisher.

Cover design by: Sebastian Podesser

FOREWORD

In an ever-evolving world, driven by relentless technological advancements, I find myself captivated by the sheer potential of artificial intelligence (AI). My fascination with technology and AI has led me on a journey of exploration, discovery, and understanding. This journey has brought forth a profound realization: It is not AI that will replace people, but rather those who use AI wisely will inevitably replace those who do not.

The rapid pace of AI development has undeniably transformed the way we live, work, and interact with one another. As a testament to our indomitable human spirit, we have continuously harnessed the power of AI to make our lives more efficient, productive, and meaningful. Yet, while we stand at the precipice of a new era, it is essential that we embrace AI with a sense of responsibility and foresight.

This book serves as a guide to unlocking the full potential of AI in our daily lives, from personal productivity to professional use-cases and creative applications. It delves into the intricacies of AI language models, ethical considerations, and the future of AI communication. By exploring advanced techniques and understanding the limitations of AI, we learn how to wield this powerful tool with precision and skill.

As we embark on this journey together, I encourage you,

dear reader, to approach AI with curiosity and an open mind. It is only by acknowledging the transformative power of AI and harnessing it wisely that we can shape a future of boundless opportunities, a future where we not only coexist with AI but thrive alongside it. In the end, it is our collective responsibility to ensure that AI becomes an enabler of progress and a catalyst for positive change.

So let us venture forth, eager to embrace the possibilities that lie ahead, and remember that it is not AI that stands to replace us; it is our own ingenuity and adaptability that will determine our success in the age of artificial intelligence.

Sebastian Podesser

CONTENTS

Title Page
Copyright
Foreword
Introduction — 1
Understanding AI Language Model — 9
Principles of Effective AI Communication — 16
Prompting Techniques — 24
Prompt Examples — 41
AI in Everyday Applications — 47
Troubleshooting AI Responses — 53
Advanced AI Communication Techniques — 58
The Future of AI Communication — 67
Conclusion — 76
Appendices — 81

INTRODUCTION

Are you interested in exploring the field of prompt design but don't know where to start? If so, you're in the right place! This book takes you right into that world. What you will learn:

1. **Comprehensive understanding of AI language models**, including their development, capabilities, and limitations.
2. **Effective AI communication techniques and strategies**, including various prompting techniques and frameworks to optimize user interaction with AI models.
3. **A wide range of practical applications of AI in everyday life**, professional use-cases, and creative endeavors, with insights on how to make the most of AI tools.
4. **Troubleshooting and refining AI-generated content**, addressing common issues, and implementing iterative improvement strategies for better outcomes.
5. **Exploring the future of AI communication**, ethical considerations, and how to harness AI's potential responsibly for personal and professional growth.

This book is for individuals, professionals, and enthusiasts who are interested in harnessing the power of AI for improved communication and productivity. Whether you are a content creator, marketer, developer, or simply curious about the practical applications of AI language models, this book caters to a wide range of readers. The content is designed to be accessible and informative for beginners while also offering valuable insights and advanced techniques for those already familiar with AI-driven tools. By understanding and utilizing AI effectively, readers from various backgrounds will be able to unlock new opportunities and excel in their respective fields.

Prompt Design Vs. Prompt Engineering

Both "prompt design" and "prompt engineering" refer to the process of writing effective instructions for AI language models, which is the same thing. Although they share similarities, they differ in their scope and goals. Let's talk about the differences between these two ideas and figure out what they mean for AI communication.

Prompt Design:

Prompt design is about coming up with creative ways to ask questions or give instructions that get the response you want from an AI language model. It involves understanding the model's capabilities and limitations and tailoring the prompts accordingly. The main goal of prompt design is to get the AI to give answers that are correct, relevant, and make sense.

Key aspects of prompt design include:

1. Clarity and conciseness
2. Context and background information
3. Specifying the desired format and structure
4. Iterative refinement of AI-generated content

Prompt Engineering:

On the other hand, prompt engineering is a more technical and systematic way to improve how the user and the AI model work together. It involves looking at the structure, wording, and other parts of the prompt and making small changes to improve the model's performance and reduce problems like biases or mistakes. Prompt engineering often requires a deeper understanding of the underlying AI model, as well as the use of data-driven techniques and experimentation.

Key aspects of prompt engineering include:

1. Systematic testing and evaluation
2. Data-driven optimization
3. Model fine-tuning and customization
4. Integration with other tools and services

In the end, prompt design and prompt engineering are two processes that work together to help users get the most out of AI language models. While prompt design focuses on making instructions that work well with the AI's skills, prompt engineering focuses on improving the performance and reliability of these instructions through technical optimization.

Why should you care about prompt design?

Prompt Design plays a crucial role in maximizing the potential of AI language models and ensuring their effectiveness in various applications. For example, if you spend hours each week writing emails, reports, or code, an AI system can help you streamline this process.

This book is not about Prompt Engineering.
Experts in natural language processing (NLP), machine learning (ML), and computer programming will thrive in the Prompt Engineering environment.

This book is about Prompt Design.
People who are technically savvy but who see themselves more as an AI user who aspires to become an advanced AI user will benefit most from Prompt Design.

The Importance Of Effective Communication With Ai

In today's fast-paced technological world, Artificial Intelligence (AI) plays an increasingly vital role in our daily lives. From digital assistants and chatbots to machine learning algorithms and natural language processing, AI systems have transformed how we interact with technology. As AI language models advance, the significance of effective communication with AI becomes paramount.

Mastering communication with AI allows us to exploit these systems' full potential, optimizing their benefits while minimizing risks associated with misinterpretation or misunderstandings. Whether employing AI for personal productivity or professional purposes, effective communication is crucial for attaining desired results.

A primary motivation for refining communication with AI is enhancing user experience. As AI sophistication grows, users inevitably expect seamless and efficient interactions. Ensuring AI systems accurately understand and respond to inputs not only elevates satisfaction but also fosters trust in technology.

Streamlined communication with AI also saves time and effort. By offering clear and concise directions, users can decrease the typical back-and-forth related to AI-generated content, lessening the need for manual intervention and refining AI outputs. This efficiency is vital in professional environments where time is often scarce.

Another significant advantage of effective communication with AI is reducing errors and inaccuracies. AI language models, while potent, are not faultless. They occasionally generate vague, ambiguous, or outdated content. Effectively communicating with AI guides the system to provide more accurate, contextually relevant information, decreasing the likelihood of misinformation or misinterpretation.

Additionally, adept communication with AI helps users explore the full spectrum of AI's capabilities. A user proficient in communicating with AI can access the system's potential to generate creative and innovative content, pushing the boundaries of AI's accomplishments.

Lastly, effective communication with AI fosters responsible and ethical AI usage. As AI systems become more ingrained in our lives, concerns about fairness, privacy, and security naturally emerge. By learning how to communicate responsibly with AI, users can mitigate risks associated with biases, privacy breaches, or other ethical issues.

In conclusion, the importance of effective AI communication is indisputable. Mastering communication with these systems is essential for optimizing user experience, conserving time and effort, reducing errors, unlocking AI's full potential, and promoting responsible and ethical AI usage as AI technology progresses and becomes more widespread. With the right knowledge and skills, users can harness the power of AI language models, opening a world of opportunities that may have previously seemed unattainable.

Scope And Objective Of The Book

In this book, my objective is to equip both technical and non-technical readers with a comprehensive guide on prompt design, enabling more productive and meaningful interactions with AI systems. We will cover the fundamentals of effective prompt design, easy-to-use methods, and essential ethical considerations associated with AI and prompt design.

This manual encompasses crucial topics in AI and communication, such as the foundations of AI language models, efficient prompting methods, and practical applications. It spans everything from basic principles of AI communication to advanced techniques and future developments, catering to individuals with varying levels of AI knowledge.

We will investigate the complexities of AI language models, examining their capabilities and limitations while addressing the ethical implications of AI use. Furthermore, the book offers practical advice on crafting effective prompts and troubleshooting common issues.

The book demonstrates how AI can be integrated into daily life, professional environments, and creative endeavors. As the field of AI continues to advance, my aim is to provide you with the skills necessary to adapt and excel in this dynamic landscape.

Brief History Of Ai And Language Models

The field of artificial intelligence has come a long way since its inception in the mid-20th century. The idea of imitating human intelligence in machines served as an inspiration for early AI researchers, who used it to create a variety of problem-solving algorithms and rule-based systems. However, it wasn't until the advent of machine learning and natural language processing (NLP) that AI started to make significant strides in understanding and generating human-like text.

The 1950s and 1960s marked the first wave of AI research, with notable projects like the General Problem Solver and ELIZA, an early chatbot that simulated human conversation through pattern matching. Even though these early systems showed how AI could work, they were severely limited by their lack of computing power and the fact that they were built around rules.

In the 1980s, AI research moved toward connectionist models, such as neural networks, which were loosely based on the human brain. This change in approach paved the way for the development of more advanced language models. In the early 2000s, statistical methods became prevalent in NLP, leading to the creation of models that leveraged vast amounts of text data to make predictions about language.

The introduction of deep learning techniques in the 2010s revolutionized NLP, giving rise to powerful AI language models capable of generating coherent and contextually relevant text. One of the earliest and most influential deep learning models for NLP was the recurrent neural network (RNN), which enabled models to process sequences of text and maintain context over time. Later, models like the Long Short-Term Memory (LSTM) and the Transformer architecture further advanced the field.

In recent years, the Transformer architecture has become the foundation for state-of-the-art language models like OpenAI's GPT series. These models have demonstrated an unprecedented ability to generate human-like text, understand context, and even perform tasks that require reasoning and problem-solving skills.

As AI language models continue to advance, they are becoming increasingly integrated into our daily lives, powering applications like chatbots, personal assistants, content generation, and more. Understanding the history of AI and language models provides valuable context for appreciating the impressive capabilities of modern AI systems and the exciting potential they hold for the future.

In the next chapter, we'll learn more about how AI language models work. We'll look at their architecture, how they're trained, and any ethical concerns.

UNDERSTANDING AI LANGUAGE MODEL

A. Overview Of Ai Language Models

i. List of large language models

Model	Release Date	Developer	Number of parameters	Corpus size
BERT	2018	Google	340 million	3.3 billion words
GPT-2	2019	OpenAI	1.5 billion	~10 billion tokens
GPT-3	2020	OpenAI	175 billion	499 billion tokens
GPT-Neo	2021	EleutherAI	2.7 billion	825 GiB
GPT-J	2021	EleutherAI	6 billion	825 GiB
Megatron-Turing NLG	2021	Microsoft and Nvidia	530 billion	338.6 billion tokens
Ernie 3.0 Titan	2021	Baidu	260 billion	4 Tb
Claude	2021	Anthropic	52 billion	400 billion tokens
GLaM (Generalist Language Model)	2021	Google	1.2 trillion	1.6 trillion tokens
Gopher	2021	DeepMind	280 billion	300 billion tokens
LaMDA (Language Models for Dialog Applications	2022	Google	137 billion	1.56T words, 168 billion tokens
GPT-NeoX	2022	EleutherAI	20 billion	825 GiB
Chinchilla	2022	DeepMind	70 billion	1.4 trillion tokens
PaLM (Pathways Language Model)	2022	Google	540 billion	768 billion tokens
OPT (Open Pretrained Transformer)	2022	Meta	175 billion	180 billion tokens

YaLM 100B	2022	Yandex	100 billion	1.7TB
Minerva	2022	Google	540 billion	38.5B tokens from webpages filtered for mathematical content and from papers submitted to the arXiv preprint server
BLOOM	2022	Large collaboration led by Hugging Face	175 billion	350 billion tokens
AlexaTM (Teacher Models)	2022	Amazon	20 billion	1.3 trillion
LLaMA (Large Language Model Meta AI)	2023	Meta	65 billion	1.4 trillion
Luminous	2023	AlephAlpha	13 billion	?
GPT-4	2023	OpenAI	?	?
Cerebras-GPT	2023	Cerebras	13 billion	?
Bard	2023	Google	?	?

Sources:
https://en.wikipedia.org/wiki/Large_language_model
https://medium.com/aleph-alpha-blog/luminous-explore-a-model-for-world-class-semantic-representation-f1b856261a2

ii. Limitations and capabilities

AI language models have demonstrated remarkable capabilities, but they also have limitations that users must be aware of when interacting with them.

Capabilities:

Generating coherent and contextually relevant text: Modern language models like GPT-4 can generate text that closely resembles human writing in terms of coherence, style, and context.

Adapting to different tasks: AI language models can perform a variety of tasks, including text generation, translation, summarization, sentiment analysis, and more.

Understanding and following instructions: When provided with clear instructions, these models can produce text that adheres to the given constraints or requirements.

Learning from examples: AI language models can learn from examples provided in the input, allowing them to adapt their output to specific formats or styles.

Limitations:

Lack of common sense and reasoning: AI language models sometimes produce output that lacks common sense or demonstrates flawed reasoning, as they are primarily trained on text patterns and not on a deep understanding of the world.

Inaccurate or outdated information: Language models rely on the text data they were trained on, which may contain inaccuracies, biases, or outdated information. As a result, their output may sometimes be incorrect or misleading.

Sensitivity to input phrasing: The output generated by AI language models can be sensitive to the phrasing of the input prompt, which means that slight changes in the prompt might lead to different results.

Ethical concerns: AI language models may inadvertently generate biased, offensive, or inappropriate content based on the text data they were trained on, raising ethical concerns.

Understanding the capabilities and limitations of AI language models is essential for using them effectively and responsibly. In the following sections, we will explore in more detail how these models are trained and the ethical considerations associated with their use.

B. Training And Data Processing

i. Training datasets

Training datasets play a crucial role in the development of AI language models. They consist of vast amounts of text data that are used to teach the model the structure and patterns of natural language. The quality, variety, and size of the training dataset have a direct effect on how well the model can understand and create text that looks like it was written by a person.

AI language models usually get their training data from a wide range of online texts, like websites, books, articles, and other written content. This diverse range of sources ensures that the model is exposed to different styles, topics, and perspectives, enabling it to generate more coherent and contextually relevant text.

However, the training data may also contain biases, inaccuracies, or outdated information, which can affect the model's output. To mitigate these issues, the dataset must be carefully curated, and potential biases should be addressed during the model's development.

Some AI language models use unsupervised learning, which means they are trained on raw text data without any additional annotations or labels. This allows the model to learn the structure and patterns of language by analyzing the statistical properties of the text. Other models may employ supervised learning, using annotated datasets with labeled examples for specific tasks such as sentiment analysis or named entity recognition.

ii. Fine-tuning

Fine-tuning is a crucial step in the development of AI language models that helps tailor their performance for specific tasks or domains. After pre-training on large-scale datasets, the models are fine-tuned on smaller, task-specific datasets to adapt their knowledge and capabilities to the desired use case.

Fine-tuning is an iterative process that involves changing the model's parameters based on the task-specific dataset. During this process, the model is exposed to examples of the target task and learns to make predictions or generate text that aligns with the task's requirements.

There are several benefits to fine-tuning AI language models. First, it helps the model do better on certain tasks by taking advantage of what it already knows and adapting it to the task at hand. Second, it lets users make AI models that are specific to their needs or the language of their industry. This makes the model more useful and effective.

Fine-tuning can be performed using various techniques, including transfer learning and domain adaptation. Transfer learning involves using a pre-trained model as a starting point and then training it further on a task-specific dataset. Domain adaptation, on the other hand, focuses on adapting a model trained in one domain to perform well in a different but related domain.

C. Ethics And Ai Use

i. Bias and fairness

As has been mentioned several times in this book, AI language models can unwittingly learn and propagate the biases present in the texts they are trained on. Bias in AI language models can manifest in several ways, including through gender, racial, or cultural biases, which may lead to unfair or discriminatory outcomes.

This can lead to several negative consequences, such as perpetuating stereotypes, reinforcing harmful beliefs, or producing content that is offensive or inappropriate. To address these issues, it is crucial to develop AI language models with fairness and inclusivity in mind.

Several approaches can be taken to mitigate bias in AI language models:

Diverse and representative training data: Making sure that the training data includes a sample of texts that are both different and representative can help get rid of biases. This means including texts from various sources, time periods, and perspectives, as well as from different demographic groups.

Bias identification and mitigation techniques: Researchers and developers can employ techniques to identify and mitigate biases in the model's output, such as analyzing the generated text for potential biases and refining the model accordingly.

Transparent evaluation metrics: Developing clear and transparent evaluation metrics can help identify and address potential biases in AI language models. These metrics should consider fairness and inclusivity alongside other performance measures.

Ongoing monitoring and updates: Continuously monitoring the AI language model's output and updating its training data and algorithms can help keep biases in check and ensure that the model remains fair and inclusive over time.

ii. Privacy and security

As AI language models become more sophisticated and are integrated into various applications, concerns about privacy and security become increasingly important. The use of AI language models can raise several privacy and security-related concerns, including data privacy, model security, and potential misuse.

Data privacy: AI language models are trained on vast amounts of text data, some of which may contain sensitive or personally identifiable information (PII). Ensuring that the training data is anonymized and free of PII is crucial for maintaining user privacy.

Model security: Ensuring the security of AI language models and the systems they are deployed in is vital for preventing unauthorized access, tampering, or misuse. This may involve implementing strong authentication and authorization mechanisms, as well as monitoring and auditing the AI system's usage.

Potential misuse: AI language models have the potential to be misused for malicious purposes, such as generating fake news, disinformation, or harmful content. To mitigate the risk of misuse, developers and users should establish guidelines and policies governing the responsible use of AI language models and implement monitoring systems to detect and prevent misuse.

Privacy and security concerns in AI language models are a constant challenge that researchers, developers, and users must work together to solve. By adopting best practices and maintaining an ethical approach, we can help ensure that AI language models are used responsibly and for the benefit of all.

In the next chapter, we will discuss the principles of effective AI communication, which will serve as a foundation for learning how to design prompts and interact with AI language models effectively.

PRINCIPLES OF EFFECTIVE AI COMMUNICATION

A. Clear And Concise Prompts

One of the fundamental principles of effective AI communication is crafting clear and concise prompts. When interacting with AI language models, the quality of the input prompt has a significant impact on the quality of the generated output. By providing a clear and concise prompt, you increase the likelihood of receiving the desired response from the AI.

Clear prompts help AI language models understand the context and intent of your request, enabling them to generate more relevant and accurate output. To create clear prompts, consider the following guidelines:

Specify your goal: Clearly state the purpose or objective of your request, so the AI model knows what kind of information or output you are seeking. This may involve specifying the type of content you want, the format you prefer, or any other relevant details.

Be concise: Use simple and straightforward language to convey your request. Avoid using overly complex sentences or unnecessary jargon, which may confuse the AI model or lead to ambiguous interpretations.

Use proper grammar and punctuation: AI language models are sensitive to grammar and punctuation, so using proper language structure can help them better understand your prompt and generate more accurate responses.

Disambiguate when needed: If your prompt contains terms or concepts that might be ambiguous or have multiple meanings, provide additional context to clarify your intended meaning.

Define any constraints or requirements: If your request has specific constraints or requirements, such as a word count, deadline, or style, make sure to include this information in your prompt. This will help the AI model tailor its output to meet your expectations.

By following these guidelines, you can create clear and concise prompts that enable AI language models to generate more accurate, relevant, and useful output. In the next two chapters "Prompt Techniques" and "Prompt Examples" you can expect very concrete prompt techniques and two different prompt formulas with examples.

B. Context And Background Information

Providing context and background information is another essential principle of effective AI communication. AI language models rely on the information provided in the prompt to generate relevant and accurate output. By including sufficient context and background information in your prompt, you can help the AI model better understand your request and produce more targeted responses.

Here are some tips for providing context and background information in your prompts:

a. Set the stage:

<u>Tip:</u> Give a short description of the situation or scenario your request is about, especially if it has to do with a specific domain, industry, or topic.

<u>Example:</u> "Imagine you are writing an article for a technology blog about the latest advancements in electric vehicle battery technology."

b. Explain key concepts:

<u>Tip:</u> If your request involves complex or specialized concepts, take a moment to explain them in your prompt.

<u>Example:</u> "Please summarize the main ideas of quantum computing, a field of study that focuses on the development of computer-based technologies centered around the principles of quantum theory, which explains the behavior of energy and material on the smallest (atomic and subatomic) scales."

c. Provide examples:

<u>Tip:</u> Using examples in your prompt can help the AI model understand what you want and come up with similar content.

<u>Example</u>: "Write a product description for a new smartphone, similar to how Apple describes their iPhones, focusing on its sleek design, powerful performance, and innovative features."

d. Include relevant details:

<u>Tip:</u> If your request requires the AI model to consider specific details, make sure to include them in your prompt.

<u>Example:</u> "Write a brief overview of the top three countries with the highest GDP in 2022, which are the United States, China,

and Japan, and discuss the main factors contributing to their economic success."

e. Address potential ambiguities:

Tip: If your prompt contains terms or concepts that might be ambiguous or have multiple meanings, provide additional context to clarify your intended meaning.

Example: "Explain the process of photosynthesis in plants (not the process of developing photographs), which is the process by which green plants and some other organisms use sunlight to synthesize foods with the help of chlorophyll pigments."

By including context and background information in your prompts, you can help AI language models produce more accurate, useful, and relevant results. In the next section, we'll talk about why it's important to specify the format and structure of AI communication prompts.

C. Specifying Desired Format And Structure

When interacting with AI language models, specifying the desired format and structure in your prompt can significantly impact the quality and usefulness of the generated output. By clearly defining your expectations for the format and structure, you help guide the AI model towards producing output that meets your specific requirements.

Here are some tips for specifying the desired format and structure in your prompts, along with examples:

1. Request a specific format:

Tip: Clearly state the type of format you want the AI model to generate, such as a list, paragraph, bullet points, or table.

Example: "Provide a list of five benefits of adopting a plant-based diet."

2. Specify the desired length:

Tip: Indicate the desired length of the AI-generated output, such as a word count, a character count, or the number of items in a list.

Example: "Write a 300-word summary of the key takeaways from the book "Thinking, Fast and Slow" by Daniel Kahneman."

3. Define the structure:

Tip: Outline the structure you want the AI-generated content to follow, such as a specific sequence of sections or a hierarchical organization of ideas.

Example: "Create an outline for a blog post on time management techniques, with sections for introduction, three main techniques, and a conclusion."

4. Request a specific writing style or tone:

Tip: Specify the writing style or tone you want the AI model to use, such as formal, conversational, humorous, or persuasive.

Example: "Write a brief, conversational introduction for an article on the benefits of meditation for stress relief."

5. Use formatting cues:

Tip: Include formatting cues in your prompt to help guide the AI model in structuring its response, such as using indentation, line breaks, or other visual markers.

Example: "Provide three tips for improving sleep quality,

formatted as bullet points:

Tip 1:
Tip 2:
Tip 3:"

By specifying the desired format and structure in your prompts, you can help AI language models generate output that is more closely aligned with your expectations and requirements. In the next section, we will discuss the role of iteration in refining AI-generated content and improving the quality of AI communication.

D. The Role Of Iteration In Refining Ai-Generated Content

Iteration is a crucial aspect of refining AI-generated content and ensuring that it meets your specific needs and expectations. AI language models, while powerful and versatile, are not perfect and may not always generate the desired output on the first attempt. By iteratively adjusting your prompts and providing feedback, you can guide the AI model towards generating more accurate, relevant, and useful content.

Here are some tips for using iteration to refine AI-generated content:

1. **Analyze the output:** Carefully review the AI-generated content to identify areas that may require improvement, such as inaccuracies, inconsistencies, or lack of clarity. This will help you determine which aspects of your prompt may

need adjustment.

2. **Refine your prompt:** Based on your analysis of the AI-generated content, modify your prompt to address any issues or shortcomings. This may involve providing additional context, specifying a different format or structure, or rephrasing your request for clarity.

3. **Provide feedback**: If the AI model you are using supports interactive learning or feedback, take advantage of this feature to help the model improve its understanding of your request and generate better output. This can involve rating the AI-generated content, highlighting specific issues, or providing suggestions for improvement.

4. **Iterate as needed**: Repeat the process of analyzing, refining, and providing feedback until the AI-generated content meets your needs and expectations. This may require several iterations, especially for complex or highly specific requests.

5. **Learn from experience**: As you become more familiar with the AI language model and its capabilities, use your experience to inform your future interactions with the model. This can help you craft more effective prompts and anticipate potential issues, ultimately improving the quality of the AI-generated content.

By embracing iteration and using it to refine AI-generated content, you can harness the full potential of AI language models and improve the quality of your AI communication. In the next section, we will explore various prompting techniques that can help you further enhance your interactions with AI language models.

PROMPTING TECHNIQUES

A. Open-Ended Questions

Open-ended questions are a valuable prompting technique when communicating with AI language models. By asking questions that do not have a single correct answer, you encourage the AI model to generate more creative, diverse, and thoughtful responses. Open-ended questions can be particularly useful when seeking insights, opinions, or ideas from the AI model.

Here are some tips for using open-ended questions effectively in your prompts:

1. **Avoid leading questions:** Leading questions are those that suggest a particular answer or point the AI model towards a specific conclusion. Instead, craft your questions in a way that allows the AI model to explore various possibilities and generate a wider range of responses.

Example: Instead of asking, "Why is renewable energy better than fossil fuels?", ask, "What are the advantages and disadvantages of renewable energy compared to fossil fuels?"

2. **Encourage elaboration**: Frame your questions in a way

that encourages the AI model to provide detailed, well-reasoned responses. This can help you gain deeper insights into a topic or issue.

Example: Instead of asking, "What are the benefits of exercise?", ask, "Can you explain the physiological and psychological benefits of regular exercise?"

3. **Invite creativity**: Open-ended questions can be a great way to stimulate the AI model's creative thinking and generate unique ideas, perspectives, or solutions.

Example: Instead of asking, "What is the best strategy for marketing a new product?", ask, "What are some innovative marketing strategies that could be used for launching a new product?"

4. **Seek diverse perspectives**: Use open-ended questions to prompt the AI model to consider multiple viewpoints, opinions, or approaches. This can help you explore a topic more thoroughly and potentially uncover new insights.

Example: Instead of asking, "What is the most effective leadership style?", ask, "How do different leadership styles impact team performance and employee satisfaction?"

By incorporating open-ended questions into your prompts, you can enhance your interactions with AI language models and generate more insightful, diverse, and valuable responses.

B. Chain Of Thought Prompting

Chain of Thought Prompting is a technique that helps improve AI-generated responses by breaking down complex questions or problems into smaller, interconnected prompts. This step-by-step approach allows the AI model to better understand the context, making it easier for the model to provide meaningful and relevant responses.

Chain of Thought Prompting is especially helpful when working on problems or topics with many parts that need a detailed and organized approach. By guiding the AI through the problem-solving process in a gradual manner, users can ensure that the AI remains focused on the intended topic and generates more accurate responses.

Example:

Suppose you want to write an article on the impact of climate change on the agriculture industry. Instead of providing a single prompt like "Write an article on the impact of climate change on agriculture," you can use Chain of Thought Prompting to break the task down into smaller steps:

1. First, ask the AI to provide an overview of climate change: "What is climate change, and what are its main causes?"
2. Next, ask about the general impacts of climate change on the environment: "How does climate change affect the environment and ecosystems?"
3. Then, focus on the agriculture industry: "How is the agriculture industry vulnerable to climate change?"
4. Request specific examples of the impact: "Provide examples of crops or regions that are adversely affected by climate change."
5. Finally, ask for potential solutions or adaptations: "What are some strategies the agriculture industry can adopt to mitigate the impacts of climate change?"

By following this Chain of Thought Prompting approach, you enable the AI model to progressively build context, leading to a more coherent and well-structured output. This technique allows users to extract more accurate and detailed information from AI language models, ensuring that the generated content is not only relevant but also logically organized and easy to understand.

C. Zero Shot Chain Of Thought

Zero Shot Chain of Thought is a technique that builds upon Chain of Thought Prompting but does not rely on the AI model's prior knowledge or training specific to the topic at hand. Instead, the AI model leverages its general understanding of language and context to generate relevant responses. This can be particularly useful when working with newer or less well-known subjects where domain-specific fine-tuning is not possible or available.

The Zero Shot Chain of Thought technique capitalizes on the AI model's ability to infer relationships and concepts from its general knowledge, allowing it to respond to prompts on topics it may not have been specifically trained for. This can lead to more creative and versatile responses.

Example:

Imagine you want the AI to write a story about an imaginary creature called "Glimmerwock" that lives in a unique, otherworldly ecosystem. Since the AI model has no prior knowledge of "Glimmerwock", you can use the Zero Shot Chain of Thought technique to guide the AI through the process of generating the story:

1. Start by providing a general description of the Glimmerwock: "The Glimmerwock is an elusive creature with iridescent scales and wings that shimmer in the sunlight. It inhabits a magical forest filled with bioluminescent plants."
2. Next, ask the AI to describe the Glimmerwock's behavior: "How does the Glimmerwock interact with its

environment and other creatures in the magical forest?"
3. Request more information about the ecosystem: "Describe the unique characteristics of the magical forest and the relationships between its inhabitants."
4. Introduce a conflict or challenge: "The Glimmerwock's forest is threatened by encroaching darkness. How does the Glimmerwock attempt to save its home?"
5. Conclude the story: "Describe the outcome of the Glimmerwock's efforts to preserve its magical forest."

By employing the Zero Shot Chain of Thought technique, you can guide the AI model through the creation of a unique, imaginative story without requiring any specific knowledge or training on the topic. This allows for more flexible and innovative interactions with AI language models, enabling users to explore new ideas and generate content on a wide range of subjects.

D. Self-Consistency

Self-Consistency is a prompting technique that focuses on ensuring the AI-generated content remains logically coherent and consistent throughout the response. By providing the AI with clear instructions to maintain consistency, users can reduce the likelihood of receiving contradictory or confusing outputs.

The Self-Consistency technique is particularly useful when dealing with topics that require in-depth analysis or when generating content that spans multiple sections or paragraphs. By emphasizing the need for consistency, users can obtain AI-generated content that presents a unified and coherent perspective, improving the overall quality and credibility of the output.

Example:

Suppose you want the AI to provide an analysis of the potential benefits and drawbacks of remote work. To ensure that the AI-generated content remains self-consistent, you can structure your prompt as follows:

1. Start by asking the AI to outline the potential benefits of remote work: "List and briefly explain three potential benefits of remote work for employees and employers."
2. Next, ask the AI to provide an analysis of the potential drawbacks: "List and briefly explain three potential drawbacks of remote work for employees and employers."
3. Now, instruct the AI to maintain consistency in its response: "Based on the benefits and drawbacks you've outlined, provide a balanced conclusion on remote work, ensuring that your analysis remains self-consistent and avoids contradicting the points you've presented."

By using the Self-Consistency technique, you guide the AI to generate a well-structured, coherent response that takes into account the various aspects of the topic. This results in a more reliable and meaningful output, making it easier for users to understand the AI's perspective and apply the insights provided to their own decision-making or content creation processes.

Incorporating the Self-Consistency technique into your AI communication strategies can help you obtain more accurate and dependable content, enhancing the overall value and utility of AI-generated responses.

E. Generated Knowledge

Generated Knowledge is a prompting technique that takes advantage of the AI's ability to generate new insights or creative ideas based on the vast amount of data it has been trained on. This technique encourages the AI to provide unique perspectives, suggestions, or solutions, leveraging its understanding of language, context, and relationships to produce novel content.

The Generated Knowledge technique is particularly useful when seeking innovative ideas, exploring new concepts, or brainstorming solutions to complex problems. By allowing the AI to generate fresh insights, users can tap into a wealth of knowledge and creativity to inform their decision-making, enrich their understanding, or enhance their content.

Example:

Imagine you want the AI to generate a list of unconventional marketing strategies for a new product launch. To harness the AI's generated knowledge, you can structure your prompt as follows:

1. Start by providing context about the product: "A company is launching a new eco-friendly, reusable water bottle designed for active individuals. They want to stand out in a crowded market and create buzz around their product."
2. Next, ask the AI to generate unique marketing ideas: "Generate five unconventional marketing strategies that the company can use to promote their eco-friendly reusable water bottle and create excitement among their target audience."
3. Finally, request the AI to explain the rationale behind each strategy: "For each marketing strategy, briefly explain how it can help generate interest in the product and appeal to the target audience."

By using the Generated Knowledge technique, you can encourage the AI to think outside the box and produce innovative ideas that may not have been considered otherwise. This can lead to more engaging, distinctive content and spark new avenues for exploration, problem-solving, or creative expression.

Incorporating Generated Knowledge into your AI communication strategies can help you unlock the full potential of AI-generated content, enabling you to benefit from the wealth of knowledge and creativity the AI model has to offer.

F. Least To Most Prompting

Least to Most Prompting is a technique that involves gradually increasing the level of specificity or complexity in your prompts to guide the AI towards generating the desired response. By starting with broad or general questions and progressively refining the prompts based on the AI's responses, users can obtain more accurate and detailed content that matches their requirements.

This technique is particularly useful when exploring a topic or concept that the user is unfamiliar with or when seeking to clarify or expand on an AI-generated response. By gradually refining the prompts, users can gain a better understanding of the subject and ensure that the AI-generated content aligns with their needs and expectations.

Example:

Suppose you want the AI to provide information on the benefits of meditation for mental health. To employ the Least to Most Prompting technique, you can structure your inquiry as follows:

1. Start with a broad question: "What are the benefits of meditation?"
2. Based on the AI's response, refine the question to focus on mental health: "How does meditation specifically benefit mental health?"
3. Further refine the question by asking for scientific evidence: "Can you provide scientific studies or research that support the mental health benefits of meditation?"
4. Finally, ask for practical advice on incorporating meditation into daily life: "What are some tips for

beginners to start practicing meditation for mental health improvement?"

By using the Least to Most Prompting technique, you can guide the AI towards providing more specific, detailed, and relevant content. This gradual approach helps ensure that the AI-generated response aligns with your requirements, enhancing the overall quality and usefulness of the output.

Incorporating Least to Most Prompting into your AI communication strategies can help you obtain more targeted, accurate, and insightful content, enabling you to better leverage the AI's capabilities for research, content creation, or problem-solving.

G. Explicit Instructions

Explicit instructions are an essential prompting technique when communicating with AI language models. By providing clear, direct, and unambiguous guidance, you can help the AI model generate output that closely aligns with your expectations and requirements.

Here are some tips for using explicit instructions effectively in your prompts:

1. **Be specific:** Clearly state what you want the AI model to do, including any key details or requirements that the model needs to consider when generating its response.

Example: Instead of asking, "Write an article about exercise," ask, "Write a 500-word article about the benefits of high-intensity interval training (HIIT) for busy professionals, focusing on time efficiency and improved cardiovascular health."

2. **Define the format:** Specify the format you want the AI-generated content to follow, such as a list, bullet points,

paragraph, or table.

Example: Instead of asking, "Tell me about the different types of renewable energy," ask, "Provide a table comparing the four main types of renewable energy: solar, wind, hydro, and geothermal, including their energy output, environmental impact, and cost-effectiveness."

3. **Set the tone:** Indicate the desired tone or writing style for the AI-generated content, such as formal, informal, persuasive, or informative.

Example: Instead of asking, "Write a product review," ask, "Write a 300-word, persuasive product review for the latest noise-canceling headphones, highlighting their superior sound quality, comfort, and battery life."

4. **Break down complex tasks**: If your request involves multiple steps or components, break it down into smaller tasks and provide explicit instructions for each part.

Example: Instead of asking, "Write a guide on how to start a successful blog," ask, "Write a step-by-step guide on how to start a successful blog, including the following sections: choosing a niche, setting up the website, creating content, and promoting the blog."

5. **Address potential ambiguities**: If your prompt contains terms or concepts that might be ambiguous or have multiple meanings, provide additional context or clarification to ensure the AI model understands your intended meaning.

Example: Instead of asking, "What are some strategies for dealing with stress?", ask, "What are some evidence-based strategies for coping with psychological stress, such as work-related stress or exam stress?"

By using explicit instructions in your prompts, you can help AI language models generate more accurate, relevant, and useful output, ultimately improving the quality of your AI communication. In the next section, we will discuss another prompting technique, guiding with examples, to further enhance your interactions with AI language models.

H. Guiding With Examples

Guidance with examples is another effective prompting technique for communicating with AI language models. By providing specific examples within your prompts, you can help the AI model better understand the context, style, or format you expect in its response. This can lead to more accurate, relevant, and useful output.

Here are some tips for using guiding examples in your prompts:

1. Illustrate the desired format or style:

Tip: Include examples of the format or style you want the AI-generated content to follow, such as examples of headings, bullet points, or specific phrasing.

Example: Instead of asking, "Write a catchy headline and subheadings for an article about weight loss," ask, "Write a catchy headline and subheadings for an article about weight loss, similar to this format:

Headline: 'Lose Weight the Smart Way: 7 Proven Strategies for Success'
Subheading 1: 'The Science Behind Effective Weight Loss'
Subheading 2: 'How to Create a Personalized Diet Plan'"

AI model can follow the progression of your request and build on its previous responses.

Example: Instead of asking, "Write a 10-point checklist for planning a successful business conference," ask, "First, list the five most important aspects to consider when planning a business conference. Then, provide a 10-point checklist that addresses these aspects in detail."

3. **Provide clear transitions:** Make it easy for the AI model to understand how each step in your multi-step prompt relates to the overall task or objective.

Example: Instead of asking, "Research the impact of social media on mental health and write a report," ask, "First, briefly summarize the key findings from three recent studies on the impact of social media on mental health. Next, analyze these findings and discuss their implications for mental health professionals and policymakers. Finally, provide recommendations for future research in this area."

4. **Use explicit instructions:** As with single-step prompts, it is crucial to provide clear, direct, and unambiguous guidance for each step in your multi-step prompt.

Example: Instead of asking, "Write a detailed guide on how to start a successful podcast," ask, "Write a step-by-step guide on how to start a successful podcast, including the following sections: selecting a topic, choosing the right equipment, recording and editing episodes, and promoting the podcast."

5. **Monitor AI-generated content:** As you work through a multi-step prompt, pay attention to the AI-generated content at each step, and adjust your subsequent prompts as needed to ensure that the AI model stays on track and meets your expectations.

Example: If the AI model provides a response that is not in line with your desired outcome, refine your prompt to clarify your expectations or provide additional guidance.

By using multi-step prompts in your AI communication, you can effectively guide the AI model through complex tasks and generate more accurate, relevant, and useful output.

J. Using Frameworks

In addition to the specific prompting techniques discussed earlier, leveraging well-established frameworks can greatly enhance the effectiveness of your AI-generated content. Frameworks provide a structured approach to communication, ensuring that your prompts yield clear, concise, and engaging responses from the AI.

The use of frameworks in AI communication can be particularly beneficial when you need to convey complex ideas, persuade your audience, or ensure that your message is comprehensive and well-organized. By providing a logical structure for the AI to follow, frameworks can help generate more coherent and impactful content.

To use a framework in your prompt, start by understanding its underlying principles and adapting them to suit the specific context of your AI-generated content. Next, provide explicit instructions to the AI, outlining the framework's structure and key elements. Finally, ensure that your prompt includes any relevant information needed for the AI to generate the desired output.

For example, let's consider the AIDA (Attention, Interest, Desire, Action) framework. This marketing and advertising framework can be applied to AI-generated content to create engaging and persuasive messages. Here's a sample prompt using the AIDA framework:

"Please write a short promotional text for our new fitness app, following the AIDA framework:

Attention: Grab the reader's attention with a bold statement or intriguing question.

Interest: Provide compelling information about the app's unique features and benefits.

Desire: Evoke the reader's desire to improve their fitness and achieve their goals using our app.

Action: Include a clear call to action, encouraging readers to download the app and start their fitness journey."

Using frameworks in your prompts can help guide the AI towards generating more effective content, tailored to your specific communication goals. By incorporating well-established frameworks into your prompting techniques, you can enhance the quality, relevance, and impact of your AI-generated content.

You can find more examples in the following chapter "Prompt Examples."

K. Differences And Parallels Among All Techniques

"Explicit instructions" and the "Least to Most Prompting" chapter involve providing clear and specific guidance to the AI. However, "Least to Most Prompting" focuses more on gradually increasing the specificity, while "Explicit instructions" emphasize being clear and direct from the beginning.

"Guiding with examples" shares similarities with the "Generated Knowledge" and "Self-Consistency" techniques, as all three can benefit from providing examples to the AI. However, "Guiding with examples" focuses on using examples to clarify the desired output, while "Generated Knowledge" and "Self-Consistency" involve generating new insights or maintaining a consistent narrative, respectively.

The "Least to Most Prompting" chapter can be seen as a variation of the "Multi-step prompts" technique, as both involve breaking down a complex query into smaller, more manageable steps. However, "Least to Most Prompting" specifically emphasizes gradually refining the prompts, while "Multi-step prompts" can be more about structuring a complex query into a sequence of simpler instructions.

"The Chain of Thought Prompting", "Zero Shot Chain of Thought", and "Self-Consistency" chapters all involve placing some constraints on the AI to guide its responses. However, the specific constraints used and the goals of these techniques differ from the general concept of applying limitations to control AI output.

PROMPT EXAMPLES

In the last chapter, I introduced you to different prompting techniques and always illustrated them with examples. In this chapter, I will show you different examples of how to use the framework method and how to let the AI slip into different roles.

A. Framework Examples

Situation-Complication-Resolution
FrameworkArea: Problem Solving
Example: "Write a case study using the 'Situation-Complication-Resolution' framework. Describe the initial situation faced by [Company X], followed by the complications that arose, and how they implemented [our product/service] as a resolution, leading to [specific results]."

Emotional Value Proposition Framework
Area: Persuasive Communication
Example: "Create a sales pitch for our [product/service] using the 'Emotional Value Proposition' framework. Focus on the emotional benefits that our product/service provides to [ideal customer persona], and connect these benefits to their personal values, aspirations, and goals."

PESTLE Analysis Framework
Area: Strategic Planning

Example: "Conduct a PESTLE analysis for [Company X] considering the Political, Economic, Social, Technological, Legal, and Environmental factors that could impact its business strategy and growth opportunities."

STAR Method Framework
Area: Storytelling
Example: "Using the STAR (Situation, Task, Action, Result) Method, write a compelling success story about a customer who used our [product/service] to overcome a significant challenge. Describe the situation, the task at hand, the actions taken, and the results achieved."

SWOT Analysis Framework
Area: Business Strategy
Example: "Perform a SWOT analysis for [Company X], identifying its Strengths, Weaknesses, Opportunities, and Threats, and provide strategic recommendations based on this analysis to help the company achieve its goals."

Jobs-to-be-Done Framework
Area: Product Development
Example: "Using the 'Jobs-to-be-Done' framework, identify and describe the primary job that our [product/service] performs for our [ideal customer persona] and how it addresses their needs, pain points, and desired outcomes."

Framework: SCQA Framework
Area: Presentation Structure
Example: "Create a presentation outline for our [product/service] using the SCQA (Situation, Complication, Question, Answer) framework. Start with the current situation, present the complication or problem, ask a relevant question, and provide the answer that our product/service offers."

Framework: Toulmin Argument Framework

Area: Debate and Persuasion
Example: "Construct a persuasive argument for our [product/service] using the Toulmin Argument Framework, which includes the claim, grounds, warrant, backing, qualifier, and rebuttal. Present a logical, evidence-based argument that demonstrates the value and effectiveness of our offering."

AIDA Model Framework
Area: Marketing and Advertising
Example: "Develop an advertisement for our [product/service] using the AIDA (Attention, Interest, Desire, Action) model. Create attention-grabbing headlines, generate interest through compelling storytelling, evoke desire by emphasizing benefits, and encourage action with a clear call-to-action."

Five Whys Framework
Area: Root Cause Analysis
Example: "Use the 'Five Whys' framework to analyze a recent customer complaint about our [product/service]. Identify the root cause of the issue by asking 'why' at least five times, and provide actionable recommendations to prevent similar problems in the future."

OKR Framework
Area: Goal Setting and Performance Management
Example: "Implement the OKR (Objectives and Key Results) framework to set and track performance goals for our [team/department]. Define clear objectives aligned with the company's vision and strategy, and identify measurable key results that demonstrate progress toward achieving those objectives."

SMART Criteria Framework
Area: Goal Setting
Example: "Using the SMART (Specific, Measurable, Achievable, Relevant, Time-bound) criteria framework, set goals for our [team/department] that are aligned with the company's strategic

objectives, and develop a plan to monitor and evaluate progress toward achieving these goals."

Porter's Five Forces Framework
Area: Industry Analysis
Example: "Conduct an industry analysis for [Company X] using Porter's Five Forces framework. Evaluate the competitive landscape by examining the threat of new entrants, the bargaining power of suppliers, the bargaining power of customers, the threat of substitute products, and the intensity of competitive rivalry."

B. Role Prompt Formula

A popular twist on prompt design is to assign a specific role to the AI. This formula consists of the following parts:

1. **Role Assignment:** Specify the role you want the AI to assume (e.g., Personal Chef, JavaScript Console, etc.).

2. **Task Description**: Provide a clear and concise description of the task or problem you want the AI to address.

3. **Response Guidelines:** Set specific guidelines for how the AI should respond, including format, content, and any limitations.

4. **Additional Context** (optional): Provide any extra context or preferences that can help the AI understand your request better.

5. **Initial Request:** Start with a specific example request that follows the prompt formula and is related to the role and task.

Formula:

Role: [Role Name]
Prompt: I want you to act as [Role Name]. I will [Task Description]. You should [Response Guidelines]. [Additional Context (optional)]. My first request is "[Initial Request]".

Here are a few examples:

1. Role: **Personal Chef**
Prompt: I want you to act as a Personal Chef. I will ask you to create a three-course meal for a dinner party of 8 guests. You should consider their dietary restrictions and preferences. The guests are celebrating a birthday party. My first request is "Please suggest an appetizer menu".

2. Role: **JavaScript Console**
Prompt: I want you to act as a JavaScript Console. I will give you a code snippet and ask you to debug it. You should provide the correct output and explain the issue in the code. The code is meant to display an array of numbers from 1 to 10. My first request is "Please check this code and tell me what's wrong with it: [...]".

3. Role: **Social Media Manager**
Prompt: I want you to act as a Social Media Manager. I will give you a social media account and ask you to create a content calendar for the next month. You should include different types of posts and engagement strategies. The social media account is for a fashion brand. My first request is "Please suggest a post for next Monday".

4. Role: **Copywriter**

Prompt: I want you to act as a Copywriter. I will give you a product description and ask you to rewrite it for a different target audience. You should maintain the product's key features but adapt the tone and language. The original product description is for a luxury skincare brand targeted towards women aged 30-50. My first request is "Please rewrite this product description for a men's skincare line targeted towards ages 25-35".

5. Role: **Travel Guide**

Prompt: I want you to act as a Travel Guide. I will give you a list of tourist attractions in a city and ask you to suggest a customized itinerary for a family of four. You should include activities for children and avoid attractions that may not be suitable. The family is visiting Paris for a week. My first request is "Please suggest an itinerary for the first day".

AI IN EVERYDAY APPLICATIONS

A. Personal Productivity

AI language models could make people much more productive in many areas of their everyday lives. People can improve their efficiency, organization, and creativity in many ways by taking advantage of what AI can do. In this section, we'll look at three of the most important ways that AI can help people be more productive: writing help, time management, and learning and research.

i. Writing assistance

AI-powered writing tools like grammar and spelling checkers, autocomplete suggestions, and content generation can help you write much better and faster. These tools can help you draft emails, write reports, create blog posts, and even develop creative works such as stories or poems.

Example: Using AI-based writing assistants, like OpenAI's GPT series, you can generate ideas, compose outlines, and receive suggestions for improving your writing style, tone, and clarity. By incorporating these AI-driven insights into your writing process, you can enhance the overall quality and impact of your work.

ii. Time management

AI can help you optimize your time management by automating routine tasks, organizing your schedule, and providing insights into your habits and routines. AI-powered time management tools can analyze your daily activities, suggest improvements, and help you prioritize your tasks more effectively.

Example: AI-driven calendar and scheduling applications can intelligently schedule meetings, allocate time for focused work, and even help you establish healthy routines, such as exercise, breaks, and relaxation. By automating and optimizing your daily schedule, AI can help you make better use of your time and improve your overall productivity.

iii. Learning and research

Language models can enhance your learning and research capabilities by providing quick access to vast amounts of information, summarizing complex topics, and even generating personalized study materials. With AI's assistance, you can explore new subjects, deepen your understanding of specific topics, and stay up-to-date with the latest developments in your field.

Example: AI-powered research tools can help you find relevant articles, synthesize key findings, and provide concise summaries of complex material. Additionally, AI-driven educational platforms can adapt to your learning style, track your progress, and generate personalized quizzes and study guides to help you retain and apply new information more effectively.

AI language models have the potential to transform the way we approach personal productivity by enhancing our writing abilities, optimizing our time management, and revolutionizing the way we learn and conduct research. In the following sections, we will explore additional applications of AI in professional and creative contexts, demonstrating the versatility and potential of AI in various domains.

B. Professional Use-Cases

AI language models have the potential to transform the way we work across various professional domains. They can help automate tasks, streamline processes, and generate insights that enhance decision-making and drive growth. In this section, we will explore three primary professional use-cases of AI: marketing and content generation, data analysis and visualization, and customer service and chatbots.

i. Marketing and content generation

AI-powered content generation tools can help marketers create engaging, persuasive, and targeted content more quickly and efficiently. By leveraging AI, marketers can generate blog posts, social media updates, email campaigns, and other marketing materials that resonate with their audience and drive results.

Example: AI-driven content generation platforms can help marketers create high-quality, SEO-optimized content that aligns with their brand's voice and messaging. Additionally, AI can assist in generating creative ideas for marketing campaigns, identifying trending topics, and even crafting personalized content for individual users based on their preferences and online behavior.

ii. Data analysis and visualization

AI language models can help professionals make sense of vast amounts of data, uncovering hidden patterns, trends, and insights that drive strategic decision-making. By automating data analysis tasks and generating visual representations of complex information, AI can empower professionals to make more informed, data-driven decisions.

Example: AI-powered data analysis tools can help professionals process and analyze large datasets, identify correlations and trends, and generate actionable insights that inform business strategy. Additionally, AI-driven data visualization platforms can create clear, engaging, and interactive visual representations of complex data, making it easier for professionals to communicate their findings and insights to colleagues and stakeholders.

iii. Customer service and chatbots

AI-driven chatbots and virtual assistants can revolutionize customer service by providing fast, efficient, and personalized support to customers around the clock. By automating routine tasks and leveraging natural language understanding capabilities, AI chatbots can improve customer satisfaction, reduce response times, and free up human agents to focus on more complex tasks.

Example: AI-powered chatbots can handle a wide range of customer inquiries, such as answering frequently asked questions, guiding users through troubleshooting processes, and even processing orders and refunds. By continuously learning from customer interactions and refining their responses, AI chatbots can become increasingly effective at addressing customer needs and enhancing the overall customer experience.

To sum up, AI language models have the power to completely transform a variety of professional fields by automating tasks, streamlining workflows, and producing insightful data that promotes growth and decision-making. By embracing AI-driven solutions in marketing, data analysis, and customer service, professionals can enhance their productivity, improve their decision-making, and create a more engaging, personalized experience for their customers. In the following section, we will explore creative applications of AI, showcasing the potential of AI to inspire and support artistic endeavors across various disciplines.

C. Creative Applications

AI language models have the potential to reshape the creative landscape by offering new tools, techniques, and inspiration for artists, designers, writers, and musicians. By harnessing the power of AI, creative professionals and enthusiasts can enhance their creative process, generate unique ideas, and even collaborate with AI in the creation of original works. In this section, we will explore three primary creative applications of AI: storytelling and screenwriting, art and design, and music composition.

i. Storytelling and screenwriting

AI-driven storytelling tools can help writers generate ideas, develop characters and plotlines, and even write entire scenes or stories. By leveraging the capabilities of AI language models, writers can overcome writer's block, refine their storytelling techniques, and create engaging, original narratives.

Example: AI-powered writing assistants can generate story ideas, character descriptions, dialogue, and even entire scenes or chapters. By collaborating with AI in the writing process, storytellers can explore new narrative possibilities, push the boundaries of their creativity, and ultimately create more compelling, engaging stories.

ii. Art and design

AI-powered art and design tools can help artists generate unique visual elements, explore new styles and techniques, and even create entire works of art. By leveraging the power of AI, artists can push the boundaries of their creativity, develop their own distinctive visual language, and create innovative, engaging art that resonates with audiences.

Example: AI-driven generative art platforms, such as Midjourney, Stable Diffusion and DALL-E, can create original, visually striking images based on textual prompts or existing artworks. By using AI as a creative partner, artists can explore new visual styles, experiment with unconventional techniques, and ultimately create innovative, captivating works of art.

iii. Music composition

AI-driven music composition tools can help musicians generate melodies, harmonies, and even entire compositions. By leveraging the capabilities of AI language models trained on vast amounts of musical data, musicians can develop their own distinctive sound, explore new genres and styles, and create unique, engaging music.

In conclusion, AI language models have the potential to revolutionize the creative landscape by offering new tools, techniques, and inspiration for artists, designers, writers, and musicians. By embracing AI-driven solutions in storytelling, art and design, and music composition, creative professionals and enthusiasts can push the boundaries of their creativity, explore new possibilities, and create unique, engaging works that resonate with audiences. In the following sections, we will discuss how to troubleshoot AI responses, advanced AI communication techniques, and the future of AI communication.

TROUBLESHOOTING AI RESPONSES

A. Analyzing Ai-Generated Content

As AI language models get smarter and better, it becomes more important to look at and evaluate the content they create. AI-made content can be insightful, creative, and interesting, but it can also be wrong, biased, or raise ethical questions. In this section, we'll talk about how to look at content made by AI to make sure it meets your standards for quality, accuracy, and suitability.

Clarity and Relevance: Check that the AI-generated content is clear, concise, and directly addresses the prompt or question. Ensure that the content is logically structured, easy to understand, and relevant to the topic at hand. If the content seems off-topic or convoluted, consider refining your prompt or providing additional context to guide the AI.

Accuracy and Reliability: Assess the accuracy and reliability of the information provided by the AI. Keep in mind that AI language models are trained on large datasets that may contain outdated, incomplete, or incorrect information. Fact-check any claims made by the AI, and be cautious when relying on AI-generated content for critical decisions or sensitive topics.

Tone and Style: Evaluate the tone and style of the AI-generated content to ensure it aligns with your desired voice and messaging. AI language models can sometimes generate content that is overly formal, casual, or otherwise inconsistent with your intended tone. If necessary, revise the content or adjust your prompt to guide the AI toward the desired tone and style.

Bias and Fairness: Be mindful of potential biases in AI-generated content, as AI language models can inadvertently reproduce biases present in their training data. Review the content for fairness and inclusivity, and consider revising any content that seems biased or unfair. If necessary, provide additional context or guidance to help the AI generate more balanced, equitable content.

Ethical Considerations: Assess the AI-generated content for any ethical concerns, such as privacy violations, offensive language, or misinformation. Keep in mind that AI language models can sometimes generate content that is ethically problematic or potentially harmful. If necessary, revise the content or adjust your prompt to ensure the AI-generated content aligns with your ethical standards and values.

By carefully analyzing AI-generated content, you can ensure that it meets your standards for quality, accuracy, and appropriateness. In the following sections, we will explore common issues in AI-generated content and how to address them, as well as strategies for iteratively improving AI-generated content.

B. Common Issues And How To Address Them

AI-generated content can sometimes exhibit issues that compromise its quality, relevance, or appropriateness. By understanding and addressing these issues, you can improve the quality of AI-generated content and ensure it meets your needs and expectations. In this section, we will discuss three common issues in AI-generated content - vagueness and ambiguity, inaccurate or outdated information, and ethical concerns - and provide guidance on how to address them.

i. Vagueness and ambiguity

Issue: AI-generated content can sometimes be vague or ambiguous, making it difficult to understand or apply.

Solution: To address vagueness and ambiguity, consider refining your prompt to provide more specific information, context, or guidance. If necessary, break down complex questions into smaller, more focused prompts. Additionally, request the AI to provide clearer explanations or examples to support its claims or arguments.

ii. Inaccurate or outdated information

Issue: AI-generated content may contain inaccurate or outdated information, as AI language models are trained on large datasets that may include incorrect, incomplete, or dated data.

Solution: To address inaccurate or outdated information, fact-check the AI-generated content against reliable sources and update any incorrect or outdated information. If necessary, provide additional context or guidance in your prompt to help the AI generate more accurate, up-to-date content. Keep in mind that some topics may require expert knowledge or specialized sources, which may be beyond the AI's current capabilities.

iii. Ethical concerns

Issue: AI-generated content may raise ethical concerns, such as privacy violations, offensive language, or misinformation.

Solution: To address ethical concerns, review the AI-generated content for potential issues and revise or remove any problematic content. If necessary, provide additional context or guidance in your prompt to help the AI generate content that aligns with your ethical standards and values. In some cases, you may need to consider alternative methods or sources to generate content that meets your ethical requirements.

By understanding and addressing these common issues, you can improve the quality, relevance, and appropriateness of AI-generated content. In the following sections, we will explore iterative improvement strategies and advanced AI communication techniques, as well as the future of AI communication.

C. Iterative Improvement Strategies

Iterative improvement is a crucial aspect of working with AI language models, as it allows you to refine your prompts and the AI-generated content to achieve better results. By adopting iterative improvement strategies, you can optimize the AI-generated content for clarity, accuracy, and relevance. In this section, we will discuss several iterative improvement strategies to enhance the quality and effectiveness of AI-generated content.

1. Refine Your Prompts:

Continually refining your prompts can lead to better AI-generated content. Experiment with different phrasings, provide more context, or adjust the level of specificity in your prompt. By iterating on your prompts, you can guide the AI to generate content that better addresses your needs and expectations.

2. Break Down Complex Questions:

If your prompt involves a complex question or topic, consider breaking it down into smaller, more focused prompts. This can help the AI create content that is more specific and useful, and it can also make it easier to fix any mistakes or ambiguities that come up.

3. Request Clarifications or Examples:

If the content generated by AI isn't clear or doesn't make sense, ask the AI to explain or give examples to back up its claims or arguments. This can help you better understand the AI-generated content and assess its quality and relevance.

4. Provide Feedback to the AI:

When working with AI language models, providing feedback can be an effective way to improve the AI-generated content. Explain to the AI what aspects of the content were unclear, inaccurate, or otherwise problematic, and provide suggestions for improvement. This can help the AI learn from its mistakes and generate better content in future iterations.

5. Test Different AI Models:

Different AI language models may have varying strengths and weaknesses, so experimenting with multiple models can help you find the best fit for your needs. By testing different AI models, you can identify which models generate the most accurate, relevant, and high-quality content for your specific use case.

You can improve the quality, accuracy, and usefulness of content made by AI by using iterative improvement strategies. In the following sections, we will discuss advanced AI communication techniques, the future of AI communication, and conclude our exploration of how to effectively communicate with AI language models.

ADVANCED AI COMMUNICATION TECHNIQUES

A. Custom Ai Models

As AI language models continue to evolve, more advanced communication techniques are emerging, enabling greater customization and personalization. In this section, we will discuss custom AI models, focusing on domain-specific fine-tuning and personalized AI assistants, to enhance the AI-generated content's quality, accuracy, and relevance.

i. Domain-specific fine-tuning

Domain-specific fine-tuning is the process of adapting a pre-trained AI language model to perform better in a specific field or industry. General AI models are trained on vast and diverse datasets, which can make them capable of understanding a wide range of topics. However, these models may not be as proficient in understanding specific domains, such as medical, legal, or financial language, which have unique terminologies and structures. This is where domain-specific fine-tuning comes in to enhance the model's performance.

The fine-tuning process starts with selecting a suitable dataset that is highly relevant to the specific domain. This dataset should contain text that reflects the unique vocabulary, style, and structure of the domain in question. For instance, a dataset for fine-tuning an AI model to understand medical language might include research papers, case studies, and medical reports. Similarly, for a model to be proficient in financial language, it can be fine-tuned with financial news articles, reports, and regulatory documents.

Once a relevant dataset is selected, the AI model is further trained on this dataset, effectively adapting its internal understanding and knowledge to the specific domain. This allows the model to become more aware of the unique characteristics and nuances of the domain, leading to better performance when generating or understanding text within that domain.

To get the improvements in AI model performance that are wanted, the fine-tuning process needs to be carefully thought out. A few key considerations include the size and quality of the domain-specific dataset, the duration of the fine-tuning process, and the balance between the general knowledge of the pre-trained model and the domain-specific expertise acquired during fine-tuning. Striking the right balance is crucial, as overfitting the model to a specific domain may lead to a decrease in its general understanding and flexibility.

Domain-specific fine-tuning can lead to significant improvements in the performance of AI language models for specialized tasks. It can help professionals in various industries, such as healthcare, finance, and law, leverage the power of AI in their daily work, while ensuring that the AI-generated content is accurate, relevant, and adheres to the unique terminologies and structures of their respective fields. Overall, domain-specific fine-tuning plays a critical role in maximizing the potential of AI language models for specialized applications, making them more useful and efficient tools for professionals in various industries.

ii. Personalized AI assistants

Personalized AI assistants are AI-powered tools that cater to the specific needs and preferences of individual users. These intelligent assistants have the potential to revolutionize the way we interact with technology by learning our habits, understanding our requirements, and adapting their behavior to provide a seamless and customized experience.

To create a personalized AI assistant, AI models are fine-tuned using data that reflects the user's unique communication style, interests, and preferences. This data can include text messages, emails, or even voice recordings, which help the AI model understand the user's linguistic nuances, recurring topics, and preferred expressions. By learning from this data, the AI assistant becomes proficient at mimicking the user's communication style and providing more relevant responses or suggestions.

Personalized AI assistants can offer various benefits to users, such as:

1. **Improved efficiency:** By understanding the user's preferences, habits, and unique requirements, AI assistants can provide faster and more accurate results. This can save time and effort for the user, leading to increased productivity.

2. **Enhanced communication:** Personalized AI assistants can draft emails, messages, or other written content tailored to the user's style and tone, ensuring consistency in communication and reducing the risk of misunderstandings.

3. **Personalized recommendations**: AI assistants can analyze the user's interests and preferences to provide personalized suggestions, such as news articles, books,

music, or movies that align with the user's taste.

4. **Context-aware assistance:** By understanding the user's schedule, priorities, and context, AI assistants can offer relevant and timely help, such as reminding the user of an upcoming meeting or suggesting the best time to work on a specific task.

5. **Emotional support:** Personalized AI assistants can also detect the user's emotional state through sentiment analysis and provide empathetic responses or encouragement when needed.

However, implementing personalized AI assistants comes with a few challenges. One of the primary concerns is the privacy and security of the user's data. To create a truly personalized experience, AI assistants need access to a wealth of personal information, which can pose risks if not properly protected. To mitigate these risks, it is crucial to ensure that the AI assistant has robust security measures in place, and users should be well-informed about the data being collected and how it is being used.

Another challenge lies in striking the right balance between personalization and generalization. Over-customization can result in an AI assistant that is too specialized, limiting its ability to handle diverse tasks and adapt to new situations.

Despite these challenges, personalized AI assistants hold immense potential to transform our interactions with technology and improve our daily lives. By harnessing the power of AI language models and fine-tuning them to cater to individual preferences, we can create intelligent assistants that understand us better and support us more effectively, leading to a more seamless and personalized experience.

B. Integrating Ai With Other Tools And Services

As AI language models become increasingly sophisticated, they can be integrated with various tools and services to enhance productivity, streamline workflows, and facilitate collaboration. In this section, we will explore some ways in which AI can be integrated with other tools and services to maximize the potential of AI-generated content.

1. API Integration:

Many AI language models provide APIs (Application Programming Interfaces) that allow developers to integrate the AI's capabilities into custom applications, platforms, or tools. By integrating the AI language model with your existing tools or services, you can automate various tasks, such as drafting emails, generating reports, or analyzing data.

2. Third-Party Applications:

Numerous third-party applications have been developed to facilitate the use of AI language models, such as text editors, content management systems, and project management tools. By utilizing these applications, you can seamlessly integrate AI-generated content into your existing workflows, improving efficiency and productivity.

3. Collaborative Platforms:

AI language models can be integrated with collaborative platforms, such as Google Workspace or Microsoft Office, to streamline content creation and editing processes. By incorporating AI-generated content into these platforms, you can collaborate more effectively with your team members, easily share and revise content, and ensure that your documents maintain a consistent style and tone.

4. Automation and Workflow Tools:

Integrating AI with automation and workflow tools, such as Zapier or Integromat, can help you automate routine tasks and create more efficient workflows. By connecting AI-generated content with these tools, you can automatically generate and distribute content, analyze data, and trigger various actions based on the AI's output.

5. Chatbots and Virtual Assistants:

AI language models can be integrated with chatbots and virtual assistants, such as Amazon Alexa or Google Assistant, to provide personalized, context-aware responses and assistance. By incorporating AI-generated content into these virtual assistants, you can enhance their capabilities, improve the user experience, and streamline customer support processes.

6. Data Visualization and Analytics:

AI language models can be combined with data visualization and analytics tools to generate insights, trends, and patterns from large datasets. By integrating AI-generated content with these tools, you can create more effective and informative visualizations, enabling better decision-making and data-driven strategies.

By integrating AI with other tools and services, you can create powerful synergies that unlock the full potential of AI-generated content. These integrations can streamline workflows, enhance productivity, and improve the overall quality of your work.

C. Ai-Generated Content Optimization

Optimizing AI-generated content can significantly impact its effectiveness and value, especially when used in digital marketing, customer engagement, or user experience design. In this section, we will discuss two crucial aspects of AI-generated content optimization: SEO (Search Engine Optimization) and content marketing, as well as sentiment analysis and emotion detection.

i. SEO and content marketing

Optimizing AI-generated content for search engines and content marketing is essential for reaching a larger audience and achieving better results. When using AI language models to create content for websites, blogs, or social media, it's crucial to ensure that the generated content is optimized for search engines and tailored to your target audience. To achieve this, consider the following strategies:

   a. **Keyword Research:** Identify relevant keywords and phrases related to your topic, and incorporate them naturally into your AI-generated content. This will improve the content's visibility in search engine results and help attract more organic traffic.

   b. **Readability:** Ensure that the AI-generated content is easy to read and understand by using clear, concise language, and organizing the content into well-structured paragraphs, bullet points, or lists.

   c. **Meta Tags:** Optimize the title, description, and other meta tags of your AI-generated content to make it more appealing to search engines and users.

   d. **Link Building:** Include relevant internal and external links in your AI-generated content to improve its credibility, authority, and search engine rankings.

ii. Sentiment analysis and emotion detection

To make content that resonates with your target audience and gets the response you want, you need to understand how AI-generated content makes people feel. By using sentiment analysis and emotion detection tools, you can evaluate and optimize the tone, mood, and emotional impact of your AI-generated content. Consider the following techniques:

1. **Sentiment Analysis Tools:** Use sentiment analysis tools to evaluate the overall sentiment (positive, negative, or neutral) expressed in your AI-generated content. Based on the analysis, adjust the content to convey the desired sentiment and align it with your goals.

2. **Emotion Detection Algorithms:** Implement emotion detection algorithms to identify specific emotions expressed in your AI-generated content, such as happiness, sadness, anger, or surprise. Adjust the content accordingly to evoke the desired emotional response from your audience.

3. **A/B Testing**: Conduct A/B testing to compare the performance of different variations of your AI-generated content, focusing on sentiment and emotional impact. Use the insights gained from the tests to optimize your content and improve its effectiveness.

By optimizing AI-generated content for SEO and content marketing, as well as sentiment analysis and emotion detection, you can create content that effectively engages your target audience, improves the user experience, and drives better results. In the following sections, we will discuss the future of AI communication and conclude our exploration of advanced AI communication techniques.

THE FUTURE OF AI COMMUNICATION

A. The Impact Of Ai On Communication Skills

As AI language models continue to improve, they will have a bigger impact on how people talk to each other. The integration of AI into various aspects of communication has the potential to change how we interact with each other, as well as how we consume and create content. In this section, we will discuss the impact of AI on communication skills and its implications for the future.

1. Enhanced Writing and Editing Capabilities:

AI language models, like GPT-4, have the potential to revolutionize the way we write and edit content. By providing real-time suggestions, corrections, and improvements, AI can help us communicate more effectively and efficiently. This help can lead to better content with fewer mistakes, which can help people better express their thoughts and ideas.

2. Language Learning and Translation:

AI language models could change how languages are learned and translated by making instant, accurate translations and helping people learn languages. This capability could break down language barriers and foster global communication, collaboration, and understanding.

3. Personalized Communication:

AI-made content can be changed to fit a person's communication style, preferences, and needs. This makes communication more personal and effective. This personalization can improve the user experience, increase engagement, and create stronger connections between people and organizations.

4. New Forms of Expression:

As AI language models become more sophisticated, they can enable new forms of expression and creativity. From generating poetry, stories, and music to creating interactive experiences, AI has the potential to expand the boundaries of human expression and unlock new creative possibilities.

5. Impact on Communication Skills Development:

AI has the potential to help us communicate better, but it also makes us worry that we might rely too much on content made by AI. As AI language models become easier to use, there is a chance that people will be less likely to improve their own communication skills and instead rely on AI to do it for them. To deal with this worry, it is important to find a balance between using content made by AI and working on our own communication skills.

In conclusion, AI has many different effects on communication skills, and it has the potential to both improve and test our skills. As AI language models become more advanced and are integrated into various aspects of communication, it is essential to embrace the opportunities they provide while also fostering the development of our communication skills. In the sections that follow, we'll talk about how AI is used in education and training, how ethical issues are changing, and the next generation of AI language models.

B. Ai In Education And Training

Using AI language models in education and training has a lot of potential to change how we learn and get better at things. AI has the potential to change the way people learn, from making learning more personalized to making tutoring systems more advanced. In this section, we will discuss various applications of AI in education and training.

1. Personalized Learning:

AI language models can be used to make learning experiences that are tailored to each student's needs, preferences, and skills. By analyzing data on student performance, learning styles, and interests, AI can generate customized content, assessments, and feedback that help students learn more effectively and efficiently.

2. Intelligent Tutoring Systems:

AI can be used to develop intelligent tutoring systems that provide real-time guidance, support, and feedback to students. These AI-powered tutors can adapt their teaching strategies based on each student's progress, ensuring that they receive the right level of challenge and support to maximize their learning potential.

3. Automated Assessment and Feedback:

AI language models can be employed to automate the assessment of student work and provide instant, detailed feedback. By analyzing student submissions and comparing them to predefined criteria, AI can identify areas of strength and weakness, helping students understand where they need to focus their efforts for improvement.

4. Language Learning and Translation:

As mentioned earlier, AI language models have the potential to transform language learning and translation. By providing instant translations and language learning support, AI can help students develop language skills more quickly and effectively.

5. Collaborative Learning Environments:

AI can be integrated into collaborative learning environments, such as online forums, chat platforms, or project management tools, to facilitate communication and collaboration among students. By providing real-time translation, content generation, and feedback, AI can support students in working together more effectively, regardless of language or geographical barriers.

6. Teacher Support:

AI language models can also be used to support teachers in their work, helping them create lesson plans, develop teaching materials, and identify students who may need extra support. By automating some of these tasks, AI can give teachers more time to work on more important things, like getting to know their students and making the classroom a good place to learn.

In the end, AI in education and training has the potential to make learning a lot easier for both students and teachers. By using AI language models in different parts of education, we can create more personalized, efficient, and interesting ways to learn that help people build skills and keep learning throughout their lives. In the following sections, we will discuss evolving ethical considerations and next-generation AI language models.

C. Evolving Ethical Considerations

As AI language models become more advanced and are integrated into various aspects of communication, education, and training, it is crucial to address the ethical considerations surrounding their use. As with any technology, AI has the potential to both improve and disrupt our lives, making it essential to understand and address the ethical concerns that arise. In this section, we'll talk about how AI is changing how we think about ethics in communication.

1. Bias and Fairness:

AI language models are trained on vast amounts of data, which may include biases present in the source material. These biases can be unintentionally perpetuated by the AI, leading to unfair outcomes or reinforcing existing stereotypes. To address this issue, it is essential to ensure that AI models are trained on diverse and representative data, as well as to develop techniques to identify and mitigate biases in AI-generated content.

2. Privacy and Security:

The use of AI in communication raises concerns about privacy and security. AI models may inadvertently reveal sensitive information, generate inappropriate content, or be used maliciously to manipulate users or spread misinformation. To mitigate these risks, it is crucial to implement robust privacy and security measures, as well as to educate users about the potential risks associated with AI-generated content.

3. Accountability and Transparency:

As AI becomes more integrated into our communication systems, it is essential to ensure that there is accountability and transparency in how AI-generated content is created and used. This includes developing clear guidelines and policies around AI use as well as creating mechanisms for users to provide feedback and report concerns about AI-generated content.

4. Impact on Human Skills and Employment:

The increasing use of AI in communication raises concerns about the potential impact on human skills and employment. As AI takes on more tasks traditionally performed by humans, there is a risk that individuals may become less inclined to develop their communication skills or that certain jobs may become obsolete. To address this concern, it's important to find a balance between using AI-generated content and improving our communication skills. We should also look into ways to integrate AI into the workforce in a way that helps people learn new skills and find jobs.

5. Digital Divide:

Widespread use of AI in communication could make the digital divide worse because people who don't have access to AI may be at a disadvantage in terms of communication, education, and job opportunities. To address this issue, it is crucial to ensure that access to AI technologies is equitable and that efforts are made to bridge the digital divide.

In conclusion, there are many things to think about when it comes to ethics and AI in communication, and these things are always changing. As AI language models become more advanced and are integrated into various aspects of our lives, it is essential to address these ethical concerns to ensure that AI is used responsibly and fairly for the benefit of all. In the following section, we will discuss next-generation AI language models and their potential impact on communication.

D. Next-Generation Ai Language Models

As AI language models continue to evolve and improve, we can expect to see significant advancements in their capabilities as well as novel applications in various fields. In this section, we'll talk about what's expected to change in the next generation of AI language models and how that might affect how we talk to each other.

1. Increased Accuracy and Fluency:

Future AI language models are expected to become even more accurate and fluent in understanding and generating human language. This may lead to more natural, context-aware, and engaging interactions with AI, making communication with AI assistants and chatbots more seamless and enjoyable.

2. Improved Multilingual Capabilities:

Next-generation AI language models will likely become more proficient at understanding and generating content in multiple languages, bridging language barriers, and enabling more effective cross-cultural communication. This could make it easier for people from different backgrounds to work together, share information, and understand each other.

3. Enhanced Contextual Understanding:

As AI models get better, they should be able to understand and process context better, allowing them to give more accurate and relevant answers. This better understanding of context will make AI even more useful in communication, as users will be able to rely on AI-generated content to be more helpful and relevant to the situation.

4. Real-time Collaboration and Augmentation:

Future AI language models may enable real-time collaboration and augmentation of human communication, providing instantaneous feedback, suggestions, and enhancements to our written and spoken languages. This could lead to more effective and efficient communication as well as new forms of creative expression and collaboration.

5. AI-driven Creativity:

As AI language models become more advanced, we can expect to see more sophisticated creative applications, such as generating poetry, stories, or even screenplays. This may lead to new forms of artistic expression and collaboration, as well as novel ways for humans and AI to work together in creative pursuits.

6. Emotional Intelligence:

Next-generation AI language models may develop the ability to better understand and respond to human emotions, leading to more empathetic and emotionally intelligent interactions. This could have significant implications for mental health support, customer service, and interpersonal communication.

7. Ethical and Responsible AI:

As the capabilities of AI language models continue to advance, there will be an increasing focus on developing ethical and responsible AI. This may involve more transparent and accountable AI systems, as well as efforts to minimize bias, protect privacy, and ensure equitable access to AI technologies.

The future of AI communication holds many exciting possibilities, as next-generation AI language models promise to revolutionize the way we interact with technology and with each other. As these models get better, it is important to talk about the ethical and practical issues that come up when using them. This will make sure that AI-driven communication is used in a way that is good for everyone. In the next section, we will recap the key concepts covered in this book and offer some final thoughts on the potential of AI in communication.

CONCLUSION

A. Recap Of Key Concepts And Techniques

As we come to the end of this book, let's take a moment to review the most important ideas and methods we've talked about as we've looked at prompt design and how to communicate effectively with AI language models.

1. Understanding AI Language Models:

We discussed the fundamentals of AI language models, as well as their capabilities and limitations. We also dove into the training and data processing of AI models and examined the ethical considerations surrounding AI use, such as bias, fairness, privacy, and security.

2. Principles of Effective AI Communication:

We identified the importance of clear and concise prompts, providing context and background information, specifying the desired format and structure, and the role of iteration in refining AI-generated content.

3. Prompting Techniques:

We explored various techniques to effectively communicate with AI, including open-ended questions, chain-of-thought prompting, zero-shot chain of thought, self-consistency, generating knowledge, least-to-most prompting, explicit instructions, guiding with examples, multi-step prompts, and setting constraints and limitations.

4. AI in Everyday Applications:

We looked at how AI can be used in personal productivity, professional use cases, and creative applications, showcasing the versatility of AI language models in various aspects of our lives.

5. Troubleshooting AI Responses:

We discussed methods for analyzing AI-generated content and addressed common issues such as vagueness, ambiguity, inaccurate information, and ethical concerns. We also covered iterative improvement strategies for refining AI-generated content.

6. Advanced AI Communication Techniques:

We delved into custom AI models, domain-specific fine-tuning, personalized AI assistants, integrating AI with other tools and services, and AI-generated content optimization, including SEO and sentiment analysis.

7. The Future of AI Communication:

We explored the potential impact of next-generation AI language models on communication skills, education, training, evolving ethical considerations, and the advancements in AI technology that we can expect to see in the near future.

By understanding these key concepts and techniques, you are well-equipped to harness the power of AI language models for effective communication, both in your personal and professional lives.

B. Final Thoughts On The Future And Potential Of Prompt Design

There are those who believe the future lies in the hands

of prompt designers and engineers, while others argue that as AI continues to improve, well-designed prompts will become obsolete. My perspective falls somewhere in between. The foundation of prompt language is rooted in our natural language, making it accessible without the need to learn a new programming language. When using language models like GPT-4, prompts are composed of natural sentences and descriptions, similar to how we communicate with other humans.

This leads to my central thesis: there is little distinction between a well-crafted prompt and a well-written brief. If you can visualize and describe your desired output effectively enough for others to understand and produce results that align with your vision, then you possess the skills necessary for a talented prompt designer. So, what are these essential skills?

Analytical thinking: The ability to analyze complex information and distill it down to its essentials.

Research: Proficiency in gathering and reviewing relevant information and data.

Structuring: Strong organizational skills to present information and ideas logically and clearly.

Communication Skills: Exceptional written and verbal communication abilities to convey information accurately and understandably.

Adaptability: Mental flexibility to cater to different audiences, requirements, and situations.

Creativity: The capacity to develop innovative solutions and approaches to complex issues.

Detail Orientation: A keen eye for accuracy and completeness of information.

As mentioned in the preface, I don't believe AI will enslave humanity. Instead, I think those who wisely utilize AI will surpass those who don't. And the skills listed above can be acquired by anyone willing to learn, adapt, and grow with the ever-evolving world of AI.

C. Final Thoughts On Innovation And Opportunities For Startups

The future of AI models and the extent of their innovation largely depends on the data they utilize. The more personal data provided to AI, the better the user experience. Google, with its vast array of services, possesses a significant advantage in terms of data collection. It gathers search query data (Google Search), email data (Gmail), browser data (Chrome), GPS and location data (Maps), mobile data (Android), smart home and voice data (Assistant), video data (YouTube), fitness and health data (Google Fit), cloud storage data (Drive), work and productivity data (Workspace), travel data (Google Flights & Trips), and shopping data (Google Shopping) through its various platforms.

Apple holds the trust advantage, with users more likely to share their data for a personalized experience. Meanwhile, Microsoft is entering the competition with OpenAI, Meta focuses on its unique initiatives, and Amazon currently seems to lag behind.

This data dominance by major corporations can limit innovation opportunities for startups. Startups can thrive up to a certain market and revenue size, but often face acquisition by these larger companies once they surpass that threshold. To foster innovation, it may not be necessary to heavily regulate these tech giants. Instead, giving individuals control over their own well-encrypted data vaults, allowing them to decide which data to share with specific companies, could unleash a wave of innovation and create opportunities for startups. This approach would democratize data access, opening the gates for increased competition and breakthroughs in the AI industry.

APPENDICES

A. Glossary

AI (Artificial Intelligence): The field of computer science focused on creating machines and systems that can perform tasks typically requiring human intelligence, such as problem-solving, learning, and understanding natural language.

NLP (Natural Language Processing): A subfield of AI that deals with the interaction between computers and human language, enabling machines to understand, interpret, and generate human language.

GPT (Generative Pre-trained Transformer): A series of advanced AI language models developed by OpenAI, designed to generate human-like text based on given prompts.

Training Dataset: A collection of data used to train an AI model, allowing it to learn patterns and relationships within the data and make predictions or perform tasks based on that knowledge.

Fine-tuning: The process of adjusting an already trained AI model by training it further on a smaller, more specific dataset to improve its performance in a specific domain or task.

Bias: Systematic errors in AI-generated content, often resulting from biases present in the training data, which can lead to unfair or discriminatory outcomes.

Prompt: A text input provided to an AI language model, which serves as a starting point for generating a response or completing a task.

Sentiment Analysis: The process of using AI to determine the sentiment or emotion expressed in a piece of text, such as positive, negative, or neutral.

Domain-specific Fine-tuning: The process of training an AI model on a dataset specific to a particular domain, industry, or topic, in order to improve its performance and relevance in that context.

B. Keeping Up With The Rapidly Evolving A. I. Landscape

The world of AI is advancing at breakneck speed, making it challenging to provide static resource recommendations that remain relevant over time. For this reason, I've opted not to include specific resources within this book, as they may quickly become outdated.

However, there is one resource I would like to share with you if you would like to delve deeper into the topic of prompt design:

Learn Prompting
A free, open source course on Communicating with AI
https://learnprompting.org/

C. Frequently Asked Questions About A. I. And Communication

What is an AI language model?

An AI language model is a type of artificial intelligence system designed to understand, interpret, and generate human language. These models are trained on large datasets of text and can be used for various tasks, such as text generation, translation, summarization, and sentiment analysis.

How do AI language models work?

AI language models are typically based on neural networks that learn to recognize patterns and relationships within text data. By analyzing this data, the models can generate new text, answer questions, or perform other language-related tasks based on the patterns they've learned.

Can AI language models understand context?

While AI language models have made significant progress in understanding context and generating coherent responses, they are still limited by their training data and algorithms. Providing more context and information in your prompts can help improve the quality and relevance of AI-generated content.

How can I improve the quality of AI-generated content?

To improve the quality of AI-generated content, consider using clear and concise prompts, providing context and background information, specifying the desired format and structure, and iterating on the AI-generated content to refine it further.

Are AI language models biased?

AI language models can exhibit biases due to the nature of their training data, which may contain biased or unrepresentative samples of human language. It's essential to be aware of these biases and strive to minimize their impact on the content generated by AI models.

What are some ethical concerns related to AI and communication?

Ethical concerns related to AI and communication include

bias and fairness, privacy and security, the impact of AI on communication skills, and the potential for AI-generated content to spread misinformation or be used maliciously.

Can AI language models be used for creative tasks?

Yes, AI language models can be used for various creative tasks, including storytelling, screenwriting, art and design, and music composition. However, they are still tools that require human guidance, input, and interpretation to produce high-quality creative content.

What are some popular applications of AI language models?

Popular applications of AI language models include personal productivity (writing assistance, time management, learning and research), professional use-cases (marketing and content generation, data analysis and visualization, customer service and chatbots), and creative applications (storytelling, art, and music composition).

What does the future hold for AI communication?

The future of AI communication is likely to see continued advancements in AI language models, making them more capable and versatile in understanding and generating human language. This will impact communication skills, education, and training, and lead to evolving ethical considerations and the development of next-generation AI language models.

How do I get started with using AI language models?

To start using AI language models, you can try out ChatGPT for free.

Can AI language models be trained on specific domains?

Yes, AI language models can be fine-tuned on specific domains to improve their performance and accuracy for specialized tasks. Domain-specific fine-tuning involves training the model on a dataset relevant to the specific field, such as medical literature, legal documents, or financial news.

What is the role of AI in improving communication skills?

AI can assist in improving communication skills by providing real-time feedback, suggestions, and corrections, as well as helping users structure their thoughts more effectively. AI-driven tools can also be used for language learning, enhancing vocabulary, and developing better writing habits.

Can AI language models understand multiple languages?

Many AI language models are trained on multilingual datasets, which means they can understand and generate content in multiple languages. However, their performance may vary depending on the language and the complexity of the task.

How do AI language models handle ambiguity in prompts?

AI language models might generate content based on the most common interpretation of ambiguous prompts, but the output may not always match the user's intent. To avoid ambiguity, it's crucial to provide clear and specific prompts when interacting with AI language models.

How do I ensure the privacy and security of my data when using AI language models?

To ensure privacy and security, it's important to use AI platforms and tools from reputable organizations with transparent data handling policies. Additionally, be cautious when sharing sensitive information with AI models, as the data you provide might be stored or processed by third parties.

What are some limitations of AI language models?

AI language models have limitations such as generating irrelevant or nonsensical content, being sensitive to slight changes in input, and sometimes producing verbose or overly cautious responses. They may also struggle with tasks that require deep understanding, common sense, or complex reasoning.

Can AI language models be integrated with other tools and services?

Yes, AI language models can be integrated with various tools and services, such as project management platforms, content management systems, customer relationship management tools, and data visualization applications, to enhance their functionality and streamline workflows.

How do I evaluate the quality of AI-generated content?

To evaluate the quality of AI-generated content, consider factors such as relevance, accuracy, coherence, and readability. It's important to review and refine the content generated by AI models, as they may not always produce perfect results without human guidance and input.

Can AI content rank on Google?

AI content can rank on Google, but its performance depends on the marketer's skill level. While beginner marketers may receive limited traffic and risk penalties, intermediate and advanced marketers can utilize AI for framework and inspiration, focusing on quality over quantity.

Printed in Great Britain
by Amazon